T0129515

Love, Laugh and
Pray Always

Love, Laugh and Pray Always

Kathleen A. Donovan

authorHOUSE®

AuthorHouse™
1663 Liberty Drive
Bloomington, IN 47403
www.authorhouse.com
Phone: 1-800-839-8640

© 2012 Kathleen A. Donovan. All rights reserved.

No part of this book may be reproduced, stored in a retrieval system, or transmitted by any means without the written permission of the author.

Published by AuthorHouse   03/13/2012

ISBN: 978-1-4685-4995-9 (sc)
ISBN: 978-1-4685-4994-2 (e)

Library of Congress Control Number: 2012902084

Any people depicted in stock imagery provided by Thinkstock are models, and such images are being used for illustrative purposes only.
Certain stock imagery © Thinkstock.

This book is printed on acid-free paper.

Because of the dynamic nature of the Internet, any web addresses or links contained in this book may have changed since publication and may no longer be valid. The views expressed in this work are solely those of the author and do not necessarily reflect the views of the publisher, and the publisher hereby disclaims any responsibility for them.

CONTENTS

Section 1

Section 2

Section 1

911

Our lives were changed forever on September Eleven
When we all took one step closer to heaven
Terrorism hit America's shore
Something that will affect our lives forevermore

Although there was death, there was rebirth
For this event will make us fight harder for peace on earth
The place where we must all begin
Is to not judge people by national origin or the color of their skin

Secondly we must assure our young and let them shed their tears
Hold them close and ease their fears
We must teach them that under God we are one nation
Regardless of color, origin or religious denomination

For we must remember that our children are strong and resilient
Encourage them that their future will be bright and brilliant
If we simply all agree to disagree
The world will be safer for you and me.

We must respond to this act of terror and not be silent
If only it was possible to respond with love and not be violent
Let's show the world we mean business this is not a bust
We believe in God and in God we trust

We rejoice that the dead are safe in God's arms
Free from any further earthly harms
We must reach up to them through constant prayer
This is the only way to show them that we really care

For without prayer we are an empty vessel
Let us continue to pray and become the world's trestle
That stretches from here around the planet
And never, ever take freedom for granted

We must strop living life as a trivial game
We must realize the world will never be the same
Those poor people on a window ledge taking their last breath
Deciding how they should meet their death

God wants us not to worry about recovering bodies . . . .
For He safely holds their souls
He wants us to work on achieving new world goals
To march forward to accomplish a lasting world peace
To this terror we must call a cease.

I think this event is God's wake-up call
For peace on this celestial ball
Let's start now in 2001
We must never stop until peace is won

All we need to do is look at Ground Zero
Where we will find many a true hero
Working, digging, their stamina hard to explain
If one body is found their work was not in vain

Buildings they can blow up and steel they can destroy
Nothing will ever tumble our happiness and joy
That we have by living in the USA
For free we are and free we will stay!!

A Reason

You ask me why
But I have no answer for you now
I have to make up my mind
Not whether to stay or leave
I need to try to end this misery
Losing you is far from what I want
It would be like losing the world
It would be too high of a price to pay
But you want a reason
The reason is life
Yes life is a reason
Because it causes changes
That no one can foresee
Or even to try to fix its course
Love is one of life's many adventures
Some may never come upon it
Their sadness is someone else's happiness
I once heard that the future is a road
A road stemming from the present
This road comes from the past
It is an unknown road but it must be traveled
You cannot ignore it.
Because it is life
Ignoring life is death
You love me
You've done so much for me
I am very grateful
Don't get me wrong
It's just life,
It's just life.

Kathleen A. Donovan

A Special Bond

This group has formed a special bond,
For we all lost someone of whom we were very fond.
Was this person a mother, father, aunt, uncle, husband or wife?
Each one of them was so special in our life.

We were blessed to have Hospice on our side,
To help explain and understand the tears we've cried.
We've also learned to help each other through our grief,
A shoulder to cry on, a step towards relief.

We all mourn for a different reason,
God's healing power will cure in His season.
For mourning and healing is a journey not a destination,
God will bring us to full restoration.

Though our time together will shortly end,
We've all redefined the meaning of friend.
We've learned to help each other to face our grief,
Sadly our time together was too brief.

So now where do we go from here?
We take a step, we shed a tear.
Our loved ones are safely home, their new life begun,
We must carry on for there's work to be done.

Kathy Donovan
August, 2001

<u>Autumn</u>

I love the first fresh smell of fall
The crispness and splendor of it all
The tapestry of color so beautiful to view
The colors of leaves, the changing hue

The hillside forms a patchwork quilt
Of all the beautiful colors spilt
This truly is a piece of art
And of how touching for the heart

The color of the mountains so beautifully orchestrated
It really leaves me fascinated
It is as if they were painted with a paint-by-number set
It is an image I will not ever forget

Fall is a prelude to the winter ahead
The leaves replaced by a white snow bed
The crispness replaced by a chilling frost
And all the beautiful colors lost

So we will keep this beauty in our thoughts
We'll think about the winter naught
Let us enjoy the beauty of color while it is here
Thank you Mother Nature for this time of year!

Kathleen A. Donovan
October, 1995

For My Mom

Whenever I look up at the clouds in the skies
I can see my mother's eyes
She watches down at me from Heaven's cloud
It's then I want to scream out loud

Mommy, mommy please come home
I'm lost without you, I'm all alone
It seem it was only yesterday
It's been 24 years since you went away

Too much was left undone—too much left unsaid
Like the knitting needles beside your bed
A pile of your letters left unsent
The joyous years we could have spent

You were taken at a time when we were getting to know each other
Far beyond a relationship as daughter to mother
We were maturing as friend to friend
It all came to such an abrupt end

That terrible disease snatched you from our life
Barbara and I lost a mother and dad a wife
We thank God for all the wonderful years
That helps us make it through the tears

The day was Monday March 7
When God came for you and took you to Heaven
We were certainly blessed to have you as our mother
If we had a choice we'd have picked no other.

For My Dad

When asked what it is that makes me glad,
I say it's spending time with my wonderful Dad.
When asked what it is that makes me smile,
It is sitting and talking with him for a while.

When I am asked what are some of my favorite things,
I'll say it is the love that my father brings.
When asked who is the one that loves me most,
"It is always my father" I confidently boast.

I was deeply blessed to get a father like you,
I do not deserve a love so true.
I only hope someday I can return,
A small portion of this love I was so blessed to earn.

My question is how do I thank you for all of your love?
Can I pray to God who resides above?
With love like yours where do I start?
To give it back if only in part.

Although your love I cannot repay,
I hope you know in some small way.
That in my book you are always on top,
I am happy and proud to call you my pop.

<u>For My Husband Michael</u>

I'm so glad there's you,
When my eyes first see light.
To start a new day,
Loving you is so right.

I'm so glad there's you,
In my car as I drive
On my way to work,
It's so good to be alive.

I am so l glad for you
At 12 o'clock high,
As I eat my lunch,
Thoughts of you are close by.

I am glad there is you,
As I leave for the day.
Looking forward to seeing you,
To talk of our day.

You are the one stable force in my life,
Never a hassle, never strife.
I can always be myself with you,
Michael your love is always true.

You are always constant in love,
I can count on you when push comes to shove.
I know that you and your love will always be here.
I am blessed to always have you near.

I love and admire you,
Everything about you I love and I like.
When I examine my world,
I am glad there is you Mike.

So as I lay my head down to sleep,
I pray the Lord would always keep,
You close by my side and closer to my heart,
I pray we would never ever part.

God's Provision

There are some things I cannot do
Since October of 1982
I had a surgery that forever changed my life
At 2:30 PM when I went under the knife

I had a non-malignant tumor on the pituitary gland
I had the greatest neurosurgeon and everything was grand
He was truly a blessing Dr. Bill Cunningham
It's because of him that I am who I am

On that day I lost my sense of smell
Other than that I am doing pretty well.
I have my hearing and my vision
God has made his mighty provision

Although I can't smell it sure beats the other choice instead
Of being alive instead of being dead
I thank God for my life and every day I live
I work hard every day to give

To those who are less fortunate than me
I work to make so many see
That if you put your faith in God and Jesus
They are the ones who will truly free us.

Growing in Grace

This church is certainly growing in grace,
God has truly blessed this place.
We know He is here and always will,
Taking care of us in His home still.

Jesus is definitely moving in our midst,
By the Holy Spirit we have been kissed.
God's spirit here is ever so strong
In moving this tiny congregation along.

He's teaching us it's not quantity but quality that counts,
It is then we will see our numbers mount.
For when he moves among the truly committed souls,
It strengthens them to achieve their goals.

It is so awesome to witness His being,
Through our eyes we all are seeing.
That our God is Lord beyond any doubt,
With Him, through him, in Him we will work things out!

Kathleen A. Donovan
January, 2002

Happy Independence Day

Whenever you hear America made mention,
There has always been a divine intervention.
From the Mayflower to the Mekong Delta,
American's everywhere have always felt a
Need to cling close to our God,
In every battle and war we have trod.
So why do we continue to act as fools
Trying to remove God from our lives and schools?
When I was young in school we would pray,
And we all seemed to turn out okay.
Why do we try to make God a bust?
When all of our money states "In God We Trust"!
From Thomas Jefferson the great orator
He uttered the words: "They are endowed by their Creator".
God has been with us through every tribulation and trial,
Why do we continue this denial?
Under God we are one nation,
Whatever the color or denomination.
I think our founding fathers would be ashamed,
Of how we have misused God's precious name.
When you sing every patriotic song,
God's name always comes along.
From "America" to "Oh Beautiful for Spacious Skies"
Within each verse our Lord's name lies.
So this Fourth of July let us rededicate
To getting our priorities straight.
For if it were not for God's grace,
There would not be this wonderful place.
America—home of the brave and land of the free,
We would not shine from sea to sea.
We wouldn't know what it is to be free!
God's always been there for you and me.
HAPPY BIRTHDAY AMERICA!!

Kathleen A. Donovan

My Visit to the Vietnam
Veteran's Memorial Wall

I visited the Vietnam Veteran's Memorial Wall today,
All those young lives wasted away,
What was the reason for this high cost?
All those young men and women lost.

I almost felt like an intruder,
Not having lost anyone close.
This war was so much a part of my growing up,
I somehow felt a reason for being there.

I saw a young girl etching off a name—
Was it a brother or sister?
Was it a mother or father?
Or a boyfriend?

I didn't know-She just cried so.
She got lost in the crowd and could
not find the person she was there with.
I grabbed her by the arm
I said I was sorry.
She said "thank you",
It was at that moment I felt validated for being there.

It seems to me that if we put as much effort into preventing war,
As we do in fighting it, we would all be much better off.

THE SILENCE WAS DEAFENING . . . .

They said it was an unpopular war?
What makes a war popular or unpopular . . .
seems strange to me.
Does a mother who lost a child,
A spouse who lost their mate,
A child who lost a parent,
Does any of these folk care if it was a popular war?

FORGIVE US OH GOD.

I pray for those lost on both sides.
I pray for their families.
I thank you Lord for this wall,
For the peace it gives us.

A peace that those who gave their lives did not
know on earth,
A peace they are certainly sharing with
you now in Heaven

AMEN

Kathleen A. Donovan

In Everything Give Thanks

It amazes me what we take for granted,
How our views become so slanted.
We have so much to be thankful for, yet still complain,
We should have it so hard, let me try to explain.

Imagine not having a roof over your head,
Or a place to sleep to call "your bed".
What if you had no car or washing machine?
You'd have to hail a cab to keep your clothes clean.

The simplest things we under rate,
Like clothes on our back and food on our plate.
Let's be thankful for what we have got,
And try to worry less about what we have not.

"Consider the lilies of the field", they neither reap nor sow,
The good Lord lets them flourish and grow.
He has placed us above all living things,
Let us be thankful for all that he brings.

Kathleen A. Donovan

In The Park

There are many signs we see in the park,
No stopping, no standing—don't be here after dark.
Don't feed the ducks and geese, of whom you've grown fond,
Don't go skating on the icy pond.
Don't drink alcohol or you will answer to the ranger,
Don't swim in the water, you could be in danger.

Not all signs in the park prohibit,
You can view and enjoy the rose exhibit.
There are many things to do that you like,
Perhaps walking on the path or riding your bike.

You can walk on the nature trail,
Or in a paddle boat you can sail.
Adore the beauty of God's earth.
You can realize the beauty and all it is worth.

You can play tennis or roller blade,
Or simply sit and enjoy the shade!
Enjoy the park and all that it brings,
Admire the out-of-door type things.

Kathleen A. Donovan
June, 1975

On the Doorstep of a New Century

As we look ahead to the next hundred years,
There is great excitement and great fears.
The path is clear, we must begin.
To meet the final challenge and we must win.

In this new millennium we must work without cease,
To accomplish the final frontier called peace.
We can do it—it's within our range.
We have the capabilities to handle this change.

We landed a man safely on the moon,
A man traveled around the world in a balloon.
We have traveled to planets in the unknown,
But here on Earth we can't find a true peace of our own.

There are those who will laugh and say it can't be done,
This final frontier can and will be won.
If we simply practice and accept brotherly love,
We must never stop asking for help from above.

Let us leave this world a happier place,
A stable future for our children to face.
So on that final day we will hear "Job well done"!
From God the Father and God the Son!

Let's start this century as our forefathers did the last,
With dreams and visions hard and fast.
So when the 22nd century is about to start,
Our children can be proud that we did our part.

In bringing peace to Mother Earth,
In striving for all that peace is worth.
Peace on Earth goodwill towards man,
Is really where our forefathers began.

Kathleen A. Donovan

Shadows of Men

Shadows of Men—

        Following us through time.

Prehistorical figures;

        Joining two men,

Divided against each other—

        Yet still trying to communicate . . . .

Building civilizations . . . .

        Temples and pyramids

Made not be architects—

        —But slaves—

Distinction—

        Master and Slave?

God sent a man,

        To let his people go,

After some time Pharaoh agrees—FREE AT LAST!!!!

Freedom bells—

        Calling children from their motherland

Shadows of Men—

        Building a new home,

A country—FREE AT LAST!!!!

Turmoil—

       Trading lives from a faraway land-

Brought southward

       A life of chains and misery.

A new country "a house" he said,

       "Divided against itself cannot stand."

Civil War—

       Blacks freed from white chains . . . . FREE AT LAST!!!!

Shadows of Men,

       Reconstructing . . . .

Growing north, south, east and west

Horses
Pony Express
Railroad
Cars
Telephones
Machines . . . .

Drastic changes,

       Advancing

World War I
And
II . . . .
Again mended.
Presidents—elected
       And
       Assassinated
       ???

Shadows of Men—

  Afraid

Vietnam—

  Mothers and fathers saying goodbye to sons . . . .

Some were last goodbyes . . . .

Victory—

  Many years later!!!

Peace

The present time—

  Shadows of Men

Shortages

  Of this and that

Peace talks, documents—

  Giving this—taking that

Hope—

  Our last weapon!!

Shadows of Men before us—

Turn around

  You'll see **SHADOWS OF MEN!**

Kathleen A. Donovan

Shepherd's Heart

This poem is a dedication to Shepherd's Heart
We knew it was God's will from the start
A home to have and hold and keep
To care for all His loving sheep

A lovely haven to tend to His flock
He is their salvation—He is their rock
Lord bless all who live there
Keep them in your loving care

It took some time to come to fruition
Its name says it all—a blessed mission
The Lord commands us to serve one another
Sister to sister—Brother to brother.

Jesus said "You've done to me what you've done to the least"
Do so and in My kingdom you will feast
House the homeless and feed the poor
Let in the stranger who stands at your door

Help us Father to help those in need
Help us to shelter, help us to feed
We won't ever turn a soul away
For we could be in their shoes one day

Help us always bask in your glory
Let us always tell your story
Your precious image let us mirror
Let us every day draw nearer

To all that's good and all that's right
We will always proclaim your glory and might
In all we say and do and speak
Your kingdom is all we ever seek.

Bless Shepherd's Heart, its doors, windows and walls
Its bedrooms, bathrooms, property and halls
Bless the special people who live on Milltown Road
Let this be Your Heavenly abode

Kathleen A. Donovan
August 1, 2000

Spring is Risen

Spring is a beautiful time on Earth
As if Mother Nature is giving birth
To all the lovely trees and flowers
Warmer weather and cool spring showers

We celebrate our risen Lord
With all the love that He has poured
On those who trust in His loving care.
He proves that He is always there.

Thank God for this Spring of Springs
For all the love and joy He brings
Christ has risen from the grave
He gave His life for ours to save.

HAPPY SPRING!!!
HAPPY RESURRECTION!!!

Kathleen A. Donovan

The Aftermath

On September 16 we were struck by Hurricane Floyd
In the aftermath so much was destroyed
One thing was left intact and we all must hear it
That my friend is the human spirit

That spirit is given to us by our dear Lord
With that at hand we will be restored
Maybe it happened so we would see that really mattered
After all was taken and all was shattered

May God continue to bless all those who lost so much
May their lives He richly touch
So many lost all but the clothes on their back
Lord help us to help them get on track

Everyone's helping hands and willingness to assist
Is proof that God is in our midst
Through the heights of joy and the depths of sorrow
He is here for us today and tomorrow

Sometimes He allows disaster to bring us back to earth
To teach us not to put emphasis on material worth
I say <u>allow</u> because He never <u>intentionally</u> causes pain
Through misfortune there is always something to gain

I pray for those who lost what they worked so hard to earn
There's a lesson He's tried to help us learn
"You've done for me what you've done to the least of these"
He wants us to care for each other and love and please

It is true that when God closes a window He opens a door
Through this flood He wants us to do more
He wants us to worry less about Y2K
We should help each other and live for today

For what if you gain everything and your soul you lose?
Then what would be left to choose
We need to be in and not of this world
Where things can become so easily unfurled

For when we surrender all to our Lord
Then we worry less about what takes place in the world
To him we must be obedient and observant
So we will hear those words "Job well done though good and faithful
servant"

In Memory of Tom and Clara Beck

Kathleen A. Donovan
1999

The Rosary Beads

The Rosary Beads are such a wonderful surprise
It put a tear in the corner of my eyes
I had to catch my breath at the very first glace
I think my heart actually started to dance.

The heritage, the color, my initials engraved on the cross
Leaves me speechless and at a loss
You truly have a God-given skill
A craft to glorify and to do His will

I cannot express how much it means to me
A symbol of friendship that was meant to be
Each bead on the rosary is a symbol of love
Blessed and sanctified by God above

Every time I look at this work of art
The love put into it touches my heart
I will handle each bead with loving care
Each day for you Sandy I will say a prayer.

Kathy Donovan
1-24-03

The Tears of a Seamstress

I think Betsy Ross surely would have cried,
To see how our stars and stripes had been denied.
I simply cannot comprehend
That our government would actually take their time to spend,
Debating on such an unthinkable act to conspire,
Allowing people to set our precious flag on fire?

Think of those men and women, who gave their lives to save,
A country, a belief and a flag to proudly wave.
Consider our brave men at Iwo Jima
Don't you thing for them it might seem a
Crime for what they fought and stood for,
As they raised our flag upon that shore.
What about our men and women in Vietnam?
Are we to show them we don't give a damn!

I think it is an unconscionable consideration,
A slap in the face of this wonderful nation.
I think our forefathers would be disgraced,
To see how our patriotism had been displaced.

For every person who fought in a war,
Our flag is what they were fighting for.
For some it was draped over their coffin,
We should praise and pray for them ever so often.

What would Neil Armstrong have placed on the moon?
What would be become of s patriotic tune?
Then I think of Francis Scott Key,
What would have happened if our flag he was unable to see?

I think the situation is a pity,
Our flag can be seen from city to city.
Yet still a law we want to pass,
To douse our stars and stripes with gas.

Then to set our beautiful flag aflame,
Then who would be left to blame?
I think this would ignite our very worst fears,
It would leave a seamstress deep in tears.

Kathleen A. Donovan

Those Days

I long for those days,
They were easier times.
Of Barbie dolls,
And nursery rhymes.

When the hardest part of every day,
Was deciding what it was we would play.
We would sit on the curb and burst tar bubbles,
Oh we had so little troubles.

The heat of summer didn't bother us much,
Having a best friend, a mother's touch
Dad would take us to Dorney Park,
Where we would ride the rides and go until dark.

Riding down Route 18 to the Jersey shore,
How could we ever ask for more?
We would play on the beach and catch a wave,
If just one moment of that I could save.

Out in the street,
There would be a water fight.
Then we would catch lightning bugs
In a jar at night.

Sometimes out on the porch
we would sleep,
When we got scared
inside we would creep.

All day long we would pay games,
Monopoly, Life and Trouble.
But when the street light went on,
We were inside on the double.

If I could have one dream come true,
I would return to those days for an hour or two.
I would savor the experience and chat with my mother,
I miss her so much—She was like no other.

Since I can't go back to that time and space,
I will keep those memories tucked in a special place.
The games, the friends, the day and the night,
All the love that seemed so right.

I'll keep those thoughts in mind of
Terri, Doreen, Linda and Donna,
I'll go back to those days,
Any time I "wanna".

It was a wonderful childhood
With my Mom and Dad.
They were the happiest days
I have ever had.

Although we cannot live in the past,
In our memories we will make it last.
I will cherish those times when I was a tot,
I really did enjoy them a lot!!

December, 1992

To Be Part of a Team

It takes lots of planning and plenty of time,
To come up with a basketball team of our kind.
A more determined bunch of guys we've ever known,
A quality of pros and sportsmanship is all they have shown.

As the Friday night game is about to begin,
We will accept defeat, but we are ready to win.
Our team takes the court and they're ready to go
To play as a team is all they know.

Near the end of the game the score is tied,
"We will just have to win—We will just have to try".
Now there is one second left on the board,
Our team came through—we were the ones who scored.

Let come victory and let come defeat,
For although games have been lost—we haven't been beat.
Even though we lose, we're still part of a team.
However far-fetched or strange it may seem.

Our guys watch their temper when things get rough,
Out comes their sportsmanship when the opposition gets tough.
For they are representing our school and our town,
They wouldn't lose their cool and let us down.

Most of the credit goes to the coaches,
Who say "play as a team" as the game time approaches.
A greater coaching staff could never be seen,
For they taught our guys to be part of a team!!

We Now Salute You
John Fitzgerald Kennedy, Jr.
1960-1999

We just said good-bye to our dear John-John
Here just yesterday and now he's gone
In our minds eye we see you saluting at your Dad's coffin
We will miss you as we've missed him ever so often

The Kennedy's have lost too many brothers, sisters, sons and daughters
Now this tragedy off the Massachusetts waters
Only God knows the answers to life's mystery
John you have now become a part of American history

We know that you are safe with God and that gives us relief
But just for now what do we do with the grief?
Like so many in your family who have gone before
I have a feeling we will miss you even more

So for now we will carry on the best we can
Being better off for having such a wonderful man
You were only with us for what seems like the blink of an eye
Why did you leave us, why did you die?

Thanks to your mother you lead a normal life
You had three wonderful years with Carolyn your wife
Now the two of you have eternity above
To bask in God's glory and unending love

For this life was a prelude to the peace you now enjoy
We will always remember you as that cute little boy
You took this country's heart by storm
May the Lord keep you safe and warm

Kathleen A. Donovan
July 18, 1999

What Is Love?

What is love?
It's hard to explain,
Does it conquer all?
Does it ease the pain?
Does love come from deep inside?
Or bring out words that seem to hide?
Is it a feeling that comes from within?
Or is it a candle that never grows dim?
Is it a reaction or was it always there?
Or does it come from people who care?
Is it a gentle hand or a peaceful touch?
Or a word that is spoken that means so much
Love is an idea and we will never know,
What brings love to us or makes love go.
My answer to this all seems real,
It may be the happiness you make me feel.
I know not of love—could it just be a view?
One thing is certain, I see it in you.

Kathleen A. Donovan

For . . . . .

Poems of dedication to my friends & family

Section 2

201 Omni Drive

Welcome to your brand new digs,
A new home for you and your happy pigs!
You've rid yourself of all the bad swine,
By leaving those other dentists behind.

For here is the plain and simple truth,
Without you they would never have seen a tooth.
You made them what they are—it's now their loss,
Let them take their teeth and just go floss.

Their practice will need lots of "braces",
For your new practice is going places.
You are off on new adventures,
Their left holding the rotting old dentures.

They better learn to get it right,
For out of their business you're taking a "bite"!
You'll be growing watching their business as it fell,
They'll be left holding the toothpaste and gel!

9-24-02

42

"A Present of the Past"

I wanted to give you a present to last
So I decided to give you a "present of the past"
For I've spent so many happy holidays with you
This is the thing I had to do

So just where does one start
To recall those memories of the heart
Let's go back to the year of 1978
The "Year of Injustice", wasn't it great?

That year had a special event
That when it was over much money was spent
December 15, 1978 how could we forget?
For Mr. Ken reminds us yet

Christmas Eve always included a trip to see Marlene Wall
When Santa arrived the kids had a ball
How could we forget the killer Christmas tree?
Or the gifs from Dan, Mary and Elly

You and I posing in from of the tree
We could have posed for a laxative commercial you and me
The Smalley's were always a part of our holiday fare
With funny pictures holding the pink bear

Then there was the time we got drunk on New Year's Eve
I was so far gone I could not leave
So I fell asleep on your couch, on my head
When I awoke you had gone to bed

Of course a part of our holiday cheer
Were having our good friends so near
Bob, Larry, Daria, Donna, Terri, Scott and Willy
Those late nights seemed to get very silly

Playing charades and going full throttle
That's a bridge not a ship in the bottle
Or drinking cooking wine late one night
By that time it really tasted all right.

What is there to say Ken you are like a brother?
You truly are my significant other
I don't know what life would be without you around
In you I see what a best friend I've found

Kathleen A. Donovan
January 9, 1982

44

A Tribute to Helen

Helen was a gentle woman who quietly left this life
Now she rests peacefully free of this worlds strife
She was a "quiet" person who barely spoke a word
If you listened to her eyes so much could be heard

Her love for Kathleen, Mick, Rachael, Michael and Sean
Was so very deep and so very strong
Her eyes show appreciation that couldn't be verbally expressed
To spend her life with Kathleen and Mick, she was blessed

Kathleen you'll miss going with her to the grocery store
Spotting her gray hair as she waited at the door
All the special meals with her family she shared
How much she loved you and how much she cared

We know that God and Jesus are at your side
Because we know they too have cried
Jesus sanctified mourning for when Lazarus died, he wept
God surely cried at Calvary when the prophecy was kept

So where do you begin, where do you start?
You pack up all those memories and keep them in your heart
You can bring them out whenever you feel sad
To recall all the wonderful times you have had

It won't be the same playing Skip Bo or Spinner
However, maybe for once someone other than Helen will be the winner
Mostly we'll miss her loving face
For no one else could take her place

I'd be remiss not to mention your wonderful menagerie
Of Shelby, Spinner, Spike, Smokey, Mugs and McGee
Of course Kissee will miss you, you wonderful feathered friend
That beautiful bird will miss you days on end

I guess God agreed to quadruple the coupon request
So Helen is in Heaven and can finally rest
For without quadruple coupons she wouldn't leave this earth
I guess God gave in He knew what it was worth

So now she can shop at Heaven's Shop Rite
She can use her quadruple coupons day and night
She might even try Heaven's A & P
No coupons needed everything's free

So we'll say so long and not goodbye
When we're sad we will let ourselves cry
For there is nothing like a mothers love
We thank God you're safe above

We hand Helen back—our heart's wrung with sorrow
We'll continue to pray for a brighter tomorrow
So tonight the angels in the stars are "spellin"
Welcome home, rest well dear Helen

Kathleen A. Donovan

A Tribute to Julia

Our dear Julia we miss you so much
We miss your smile, we miss our touch
It's hard to believe it has been a year
Your love and memories are always near

We thank the Lord for the time we had you
For we would not have wanted to live without your love
Our hearts are heavy and a tear fills our eye
You are now our heavenly dove

Our lives on earth are made complete
By the family and friends we love and meet
One thing that I truly feel
Is your life was made whole by your dear friend Camille

We are given many
Dear family and friends
We're thankful for their support
And for their love that never ends

Through our faith we know that some day
We will see you again and together we will stay
During this time that we must be apart
We will keep you close in our love, in our heart

Although we can't see you or talk to your now
We now that we will someday somehow
Until then our dear friend Julie
Please know that we love you truly

Kathleen A. Donovan

A Trip to Boston Or a Weekend in Woburn

Listen my children and you shall see,
What a trip to Boston with the Donovan's and Beck's can be.
They left New Jersey on the 10th of September,
A trip these four will always remember.

They set out on the New Jersey State Parkway with diet coke and tunes,
To keep them moving they brought some prunes.
There on the Parkway toll by toll,
They named the dead of rock and roll.

Then they went onto the mottos of the states,
The little sayings you find on license plates.
We made it to Massachusetts with time to spare,
We were happy not to be in Delaware.

We thought we'd eat well—we only wish,
It started out with tuna fish.
Then started the gorging of the great Boston trip,
Went on and on to the Chocolate Dip.

Then there's that guy named Paul Revere,
To good old Ben Franklin he couldn't come near,
Ben's children numbered 16,
In the town that they call "Bean".

When the windows of the hotel fell out into the street,
The Copley thought they had them beat.
So Hancock bought them as you would expect,
Then Hancock proceeded to sue the architect.
Immediately everyone went into shock,
When they discovered the Copley to be insured by Hancock!

Then we couldn't find Hanover Street,
A little man told us where to eat.
We couldn't eat dessert we were filled to the top,
But on the way home we hit the bakery shop.

On Sunday we took a great boat ride,
We got a glimpse of "Old Ironsides"
The reason for the boat ride was really the best,
So Julie could put the coffee to the test.

The sign said food and lodging and phone,
We soon found all roads don't lead to Rome.
All roads in Connecticut lead nowhere we found,
As the four of us were homeward bound.

We then had dinner with the geriatric crew,
We found without teeth it is hard to chew.
When we thought we were done eating candies,
Bob went wild with the Andee's.

"So listen my children and You Will Hear",
That the answer is always "Paul Revere".
When you don't know the song hum the best you can.
You can always revert to the theme of Batman.

Kathleen A. Donovan
September 13, 1993

Another Happy Year

Another year, another special day,
It's good that good friends don't go far away.
This has become a celebration—a yearly event,
For each of us to reflect on all the good times we've spent.

We are happy for your and for your marriage,
We hope that soon there will be a baby carriage.
May your love grow stronger through the years,
May you experience very few tears.

The love you give out comes back indeed,
May you have all you will ever need.
May you have love-filled years along the way.
We send our blessings and wish you Happy Anniversary Day!

BAKING, BAKING, BAKING

It seems that only yesterday,
We were baking and baking and baking.
120 dozen plus cookies,
Was the amount that we were baking.

We'd stay up until 1, 2, 3 or 4
Every year we would bake even more.
Rolling that dough on the kitchen table,
We'd bake as many cookies as we were able.

It did not matter where we would mix and whip,
But we usually turned to Mr. Ken,
As long as we gave him a chocolate chip,
He would have us back again.

Upon the colored card the recipes we would write,
It did not matter if we stayed up all night.
Donna and Kathy up at any hour,
But please tell me why we bought 25 pounds of flour?

We were young and ambitious and crazy,
One thing we were not was lazy.
From pumpkin to banana and Bon Bon's Gateau,
We always remembered to write "Good Dough".

We would carry it all in a blue mild crate,
I loved those days, they were just great.
Kenny would leave us and go to bed,
While visions of chocolate chips danced in his head.

So we will take those memories and keep them close at heart,
With all the fun times we had had from the start.
Thanks for being a part of so many events,
They were truly the best I've ever spent.

Congratulations Joanne!

Dear Joanne we are all so proud,
We want to shout right out loud.
You took the challenge and headed for the goal,
You gave it all your heart and soul.

All those pounds you left behind,
Never again will you ever find.
You did all your tracking and measuring,
Now the reward is what you are treasuring.

Every time you step on the scale,
We all know you will NEVER fail.
We will always be here right by your side,
Cheering, loving you our smiles wide.

So thank you Joanne for your inspiration,
Now we are attending your graduation.
You did it for you; you did it for us,
You did it all with the help of Points Plus!!

<u>For Annette and Dean</u>
<u>On Your Wedding Day</u>

As you begin your new life together
On this wintery, Christmas-like day
May the good Lord nurture and support your love
Each and every step along the way

This is the second time around
You have both been down this road before
Bring with you all you've had along the way
Family, friends and so much more

Your band of gold is a circle unending
Like the life you will be spending
With God by your side and family and friends
May you share a love that never ends

May the love you've had in the past
Help to make this new love last
Look ahead to the fun and the love that you'll face
Always remember what brought you to this place.

Kathleen A. Donovan
12-16-90

For Ashley and Rocky

God has blessed you with a beautiful girl
She's sure to set your heart awhirl
May your life be full of happiness and health
Far surpassing any worldly wealth

Gianna will have ten fingers and ten tiny toes
She will have a beautiful face and a tiny little nose
Enjoy every minute of this special gift
Gianna will give your life a lift

She'll fill your life with love and laughter
She is your happy ever after
Cherish each day as a gift from above
And God will send his Heavenly love

Now you start your family tree
Ashley, Rocky and Gianna make three
Enjoy every moment and fill her with knowledge
Before you know it she'll set off for college.

Kathy Donovan
November, 2011

For Bill in Honor of Betty

Dear Bill you loved your mother so
That's why it is hard to let her go
Her pain is gone she suffers no more
Jesus has met her at Heaven's door

She was blessed with a wonderful son
She's so proud of all the loving things you've done
Day by day you were at her side
You were with her the moment she died

Now you press on with no regrets
For having you as a son is a good as it gets
Your mother loved you, she was so proud
Look up in the sky as she watches from a cloud

Please remember that life is for the living
You have lots more love to keep on giving
Your Dad and your sister need you more than ever now
I'm sure you are wondering "how God how"

You have shown much endurance and strength
To help your family you would go to any length
Remember we all love you and we will help you in the days ahead
We will wipe every tear you shed

We know Jesus tears came down when Lazarus died
When Jesus hung on the cross we know God cried
God and Jesus are familiar with tears.
They'll be with you through the days, months and years

As Jesus bled many wept
Through that blood a promise was kept
Eternal life to all who believed
This is the eternal happiness Betty now has received

Jesus will walk with you hand in hand
That's when you will see one set of footprints in the sand
For He will never leave or forsake
He'll carry you, each step He'll take

You will see your Mom one day at Heaven's gate
For now there's work to be done, be patient and wait
Until that day when there is no dusk or dawn
For right now you must carry on

Her suffering is over, her battle is won
Her eternal home in Paradise has just begun
God took her home, He know she was ready
Rest peaceful, rest well our beloved Betty.

Kathleen A. Donovan

For Carol and Scott

Your relationship started in cyber space
One try at .com and love took place
You each took a click of your mouse
Now you are each other's spouse

How much better could true love get
When started on the internet
That was the beginning of Carol and Scott
It was true love on the spot

The two of you took a stab at romance
You went on line and took a chance
You emailed and talked and had your first date
The rest was left to God not fate

May you be free of SPAM, Viruses and a Power surge
May true love always be your urge
May you have many megabytes of love
May your union be blessed by God above

You no longer need to look for love on line
You've found each other—it's your turn to shine
I guess you really need to thank Bill Gates
For without him there would have been no dates.

You both found your "Type" and your "Fonts"
May God fulfill all your needs and wants
May your love be "Underscored" and "Bold"
Carol and Scott to have and hold.

Kathleen A. Donovan

For Diane the Pastor's Wife

This poem is a tribute to the Pastor's wife
Who dedicates her time and so much of her life
To support her husband's chosen vocation
To share him with an entire congregation

Being the pastor's wife is not a breeze
Diane handles it with graciousness and ease
You're as important as the wife of a president or king
By the help you give Pastor Roger and the support you bring

You have formed a ministry of your own
From treasurer to baking and all the talent you've shown
So to you my glass I raise
I speak all the unspoken praise

If we put you on the payroll we couldn't come up with a price
It's impossible to put into dollars all you do for Christ
You do so much that matters and pleases
Most importantly you do it for your love of Jesus

Kathleen A. Donovan
Christmas, 2000

For Hannah Your Precious Cocker Spaniel

Hannah was so very close to your heart
That is why is was so difficult to part
In Heaven she's eating carrots and table scraps
Then snuggling up on everyone's laps

Hannah is telling everyone what a good life she had
To leave you behind made her very sad
She loved Cathy, Bruce, Ryan and Heather
Playing with you outside no matter the weather

Hannah is so special this we cannot deny
Her tail would wag like crazy when someone walked by
She loved to be petted and have her belly scratched
A dog like Hannah could not be matched

So now what do you do to fill this empty space
You remember the smile Hannah put on your face
Please know she is safely in God's care
She's happy and wagging her tail up there.

Kathleen A. Donovan

For Mary

I said a prayer for Mary today
That God would take your worries away
I know these changes have been hard for you
Please know I am here to help you through

We don't know why life brings these burdens to bear
Please know that God is always there
One thing he wants us to know for sure
To look for the open window when he closes the door

So my friend I wish you well
I know that the passing of time will tell
That there is happiness for you not far away
Hold onto the hope and watch for that day!

Kathleen A. Donovan

For My Daddy

On the second of February at one forty one
That was the day my life had begun
The year was 1992
Now your family was no longer just two.

I am love—I bring you joy
Although you wouldn't have minded a boy
I know I will never wear the Yankee pinstripes
For a while I will keep you in baby wipes

I arrived three weeks ahead of my ETA
February 2 what a day
Lots of visitors came to welcome me
They learned my name was Caryn, spelled with a "C"

I know a Bronx bomber I will never be
Maybe I'll work in a pharmacy
What I will become is now unknown
I'm sure I'll be a "hit" of my own

I don't know if I will like baseball
But I will give it a whirl
For the time being
I am daddy's little girl

You support two teams
You take no bets
You route for the Yanks
And whoever is playing against the Mets

A Yankee I know I'll never be
I think we all will surely agree
Although I'm not a boy, I'm not too bad
How could I lose, I look like you Dad.

Kathleen A. Donovan
February, 1992

For Ryan Pieter Wilson on His High School Graduation

It was December of 1983 when we first saw Ryan Pieter,
A sight to behold—no baby was sweeter.
Your mother held you in her embrace,
Your hair so red—your shining face.

You were the best gift of Christmas '83
Our "Little Man" is what you came to be.
You filled all of our lives with joy,
You were a wonderful little boy.

Although today is happy I cry a single tear,
My one wish would be that Grandma Donovan was here.
She loved you so it was engraved in her smile,
If only we could have her back for a while.

After you have graduated catch a look at the first cloud,
She'll be smiling down at you—I know she is proud.
She will be watching us from above,
Through all of us we bring her your love.

Your graduation is just one of the things to be proud about,
Your recently became an Eagle Scout.
What a great honor—a super accolade,
All the hard work you put out and the strides you have made.

As you embark on this new life phase,
May you hold fast to all your wonderful ways.
Of caring, compassion and true sense of self,
For those are greater than worldly wealth.

It doesn't matter what career path you choose,
If you keep your faith in God you will never lose.
For He is the only constant in this world,
Where dreams and plans are easily unfurled.

Whether you become a famous Rhodes Scholar,
Or the manager of a store that sells things for a dollar.
Wherever you go success will be close behind,
Because few and far between are young men of your kind.

Here's to Many, Many More

You are celebrating an anniversary
Of more than one kind
It brings back memories
Of a very warm kind

We have had you here for three wonderful years
You've helped us with our questions and fears
More than anything you have been a true friend
That we hope will never end.

Your second celebration is the anniversary of marriage
Hopefully soon there will be a baby carriage
We wish you many, many more
With nothing but laughter and love in store

Happy anniversary to you and your hubby
We thank you for helping us not to be chubby
Here's to the next one, two and three
We hope you're here with us and your face we see

We hope you know how special you are
Without you we wouldn't have come this far
Thank you for your love, laughter and caring
Thanks for your guidance and all you're sharing

To each of us you've been an inspiration
As we try to get this weight to leave
You help us every inch of the way
You truly help us to believe

It is more than losing and keeping off weight
It is you being our friend that is your best trait
It's hard to say thanks where do we begin?
If you weren't by our side we wouldn't win,
We bring you a thank you which kind of seems small
For all that you do, you give it your all.

Kathleen A. Donovan

65

In Honor of James Stanislaw

When Mary and Demeter left us for Heaven,
James became patriarch of the Stanislaw seven.
He loved his family, whom he so fondly adored,
It is now his time to be with our Lord.

Jimmy was so gentle and kind,
He so loved Barbara who he now leaves behind.
I remember him driving around with Barbara his jewel,
In his bright turquoise Galaxy that was really cool.

Jimmy always had a competitive spirit,
On any given Sunday I could hear it.
Across the street in the Stanislaw yard,
Laughing, yelling and playing hard.

I know the scriptures sing in accord,
"To be absent from the body is to be present with the Lord".
Jimmy is now safely home with Mary and Demeter,
I can think of nothing sweeter.

I know our loss is Heaven's gain,
The angels are rejoicing while we're here in pain,
We thank you Lord for all the happy years
That we had Jimmy but now have tears.

Dear Lord keep Jimmy safe in your loving care,
For we know we'll see him when we get there.
What a reunion awaits us that day,
When we see him again and hug him and say.

Thank you for being a part of our days,
Thanks for your kind and loving ways.
We will all be together with our new Heavenly parts,
In the great Heavenly yard we'll be playing lawn jarts.

We thank you Lord for the time we had,
For a while we will all be sad,
To see Jimmy again we can hardly wait
Until that day when we meet him at Heaven's gate!

With love,
Kathleen Donovan
November, 2011

Ode to Mr. Smith

Who can forget Mr. Smith and the Old Mill?
I can see him sitting there still.
He was 100 or maybe 95,
He always seemed happy just being alive.
On that little stoop he would sit each day,
To chat with those who came his way.
Mr. Smith was such a part of this place,
You could tell by the story upon his face.
One day the old mill collapsed into the canal,
It was as though he has lost a life-time pal.
We all went out to see him that day,
Our sympathy and final respects to pay.
It was as though we were attending a wake,
It felt right though for Mrs. Smith's sake.
Although I did not know him well,
He seemed as sweet as I could tell.
I could see how much he loved this land,
That's what helped me to understand.
This sweet old man, his passion and charm,
For the mill, the canal, this land and his farm.
There is a P.S. to this wonderful story,
A tribute to Mr. Smith in all his glory.
Over the canal they built a new span,
They named it after this wonderful man.

On the Shoreline

I met you on the shoreline
As the waves drifted in
The waves left the soft imprints
In the sand . . . .
It was like a dream
You were there
You were gone
I can't seem to understand
Why
Just as fast as the waves washed away those imprints
You were gone
You were gone

Kathleen A. Donovan

Time and You

It took time to meet you, I can't understand
The hours it took to capture your hand
A greater love I have never know
It was the best the love you've shown

I've never won at love before
Men have turned and on me and closed the door
Don't ever leave stay here by my side
I could never let go, this love I can't hide

Though its words I use I could never explain
To find you and hold you has eased my pain
I knew you were for me at just one glance
I knew I could have you, if just by chance

It came and I met you and now I can see
We'll always be together, just you and me
I ask you to stay would be too much to plead
You're all I ever want or ever need

If you leave I'll be heartbroken, shattered and sad
For this is the greatest love I have ever had
If you're gone the rest of my days will be blue
I'll sit here and think about time and you.

Kathleen A. Donovan

69

To A New Friend

How truly blessed could a woman get?
To meet such a sweet man on the Internet.
I really hit the Internet Jackpot,
When I met you my new friend Scott.

I logged on and took a chance,
A shot a friendship, a stab at romance.
I never imagined I would meet someone I admire,
A man who has fought in battle and a man who fights fire.

So I guess I can call you my date dot com,
I admire you so for fighting in Vietnam.
To defend a foreign people in a foreign land,
You traded your youth for a gun in your hand.

At the tender age of 19 in 1969,
A year forever etched in the American mind.
How easy it was for America to forget,
All the sacrifices of the Vietnam Vet.

They called it an "Unpopular War",
So what were all those lives lost for?
So thank you Scott for answering the call.
In the interest of peace to protect us all.

Your love of family I truly respect,
A man of your attributes, what else could I expect?
Your son Bryan really brings you joy,
He's such a kind and loving boy

You are witty and wise with lots of pizzazz,
You love Oreo's and you love jazz,
You have a special love of airplanes,
You work for NJ transit on their many trains.

A Union President, a man of the US Air Force,
Sweet, sincere and likes cruises of course.
Thank you for being such a kind human being,
I hope for a long time it will be you I'm seeing.

I don't know what the future will bring,
Although I am sure about one thing.
I thank my computer and my mouse,
For bringing you via Internet into my house.

<u>To A Very Special Person</u>

What do you say to someone
        Who has brought you to the Lord?
From childhood to through adulthood
        It's he you have adored.

How do you thank someone who has always cared?
        Who has stood by time and time again?
Through sorrow and through hurting,
        You know he will always be there.

He has made my life complete
        By teaching me the Word,
Now I am content
        Because I know the Lord.

What do you say to a man who you will miss sadly?
I love you, I'll miss you and you'll always be in my heart.

My dear Reverend Hadley.

October 18, 1984

To Honor Jolan

Jolan was a wonderful woman, who led a wonderful Christian life,
She was a devoted Great Grandmother, Grandmother, Mother and wife.
She devoted her life to serving the Lord.
She loved her family whom she so deeply adored.

Our church community will miss her smiling face,
Seeing her each Sunday in this sacred place.
We were blessed to have her for 99 years,
Now we are left with the heartache and tears.

Dear Lord please shower Jolan with all of your love,
Keep her safe in Heaven above.
Tell her we love her each day and each night,
We will see her again when your timing is right.

Keep her safe as we anxiously wait,
To greet her there at Heaven's gate.
At this moment our hearts are wrung with sorrow,
We all look forward to a brighter tomorrow.

Our Dear Miss Debbie

Our dear Miss Debbie you've been with us all through the years
You've lived through our laughter and you've lived through our tears
You have taught us that Weight Watchers is a way of life
We've learned to think differently when we pick up a fork and knife.

You do not lead each meeting by talking the talk
You continue with us daily down this road we walk
Weight loss is a life-long ride
Who other than you would we want by our side?

We plan our day – we plan our meals
Nothing taste as good as being here on Saturday morning feels
Why else would we rise at this early hour?
Than to hear you speak and feel your power

I've never seen a meeting packed with so many at life time
I know the reason and I know the rhyme
You are the reason they've reach their goal
It's because you give your meetings such heart and soul

Thank you seems such a small word to speak
But we love you and we love this meeting each week
We hope Weight Watcher's know that a wonderful leader they've hired
We hope they know how many lives you've inspired

January, 2010